Endorsements

"As a pastor, I get asked lots of questions. I'm approached by unbelievers seeking to understand the gospel, new believers unsure about next steps, and maturing believers wanting help answering questions from their Christian family, friends, neighbors, or coworkers. It's in these moments that I wish I had a book to give them that was brief, answered their questions, and pointed them in the right direction for further study. Church Questions is a series that provides just that. Each booklet tackles one question in a biblical, brief, and practical manner. The series may be called Church Questions, but it could be called 'Church Answers.' I intend to pick these up by the dozens and give them away regularly. You should too."

Juan R. Sanchez, Senior Pastor, High Pointe Baptist Church, Austin, Texas

"Where can we Christians find reliable answers to our common questions about life together at church—without having to plow through long, expensive books? The Church Questions booklets meet our need with answers that are biblical, thoughtful, and practical. For pastors, this series will prove a trustworthy resource for guiding church members toward deeper wisdom and stronger unity."

Ray Ortlund, *President, Renewal Ministries*

What Should We Do about Members Who Won't Attend?

Church Questions

What Should We Do about Members Who Won't Attend?

Alex Duke

∷ CROSSWAY®

WHEATON, ILLINOIS

Trade paperback ISBN: 978-1-4335-7227-2
ePub ISBN: 978-1-4335-7230-2
PDF ISBN: 978-1-4335-7228-9
Mobipocket ISBN: 978-1-4335-7229-6

Library of Congress Cataloging-in-Publication Data

Names: Duke, Alex, author.
Title: What should we do about members who won't attend? / Alex Duke.
Description: Wheaton, Illinois : Crossway, [2021] | Series: Church questions | Includes bibliographical references and index.
Identifiers: LCCN 2021000902 (print) | LCCN 2021000903 (ebook) | ISBN 9781433572272 (paperback) | ISBN 9781433572289 (pdf) | ISBN 9781433572296 (mobi) | ISBN 9781433572302 (epub)
Subjects: LCSH: Church attendance.
Classification: LCC BV4523 .D85 2021 (print) | LCC BV4523 (ebook) | DDC 254/.5—dc23
LC record available at https://lccn.loc.gov/2021000902
LC ebook record available at https://lccn.loc.gov/2021000903

Crossway is a publishing ministry of Good News Publishers.

BP		30	29	28	27	26	25	24	23	22	21
15	14	13	12	11	10	9	8	7	6	5	4	3	2	1

What do you think? If a man has a hundred sheep, and one of them has gone astray, does he not leave the ninety-nine on the mountains and go in search of the one that went astray?

Matthew 18:12

If a sheep has strayed let us seek it; to disown it in a hurry is not the Master's method. Ours is to be the labor and the care, for we are overseers of the flock of Christ to the end that all may be presented faultless before God. One month's absence from the house of God is, in some cases, a deadly sign of a profession renounced, while in others a long absence is an affliction to be sympathised with, and not a crime to be capitally punished.

C. H. Spurgeon[1]

Have you ever sat in a church membership interview? I have. In fact, I'll never forget my first one. Why? Not because it marked a particularly monumental moment in my life. I mean, it was just four of us—me and three college roommates—sitting on uncomfortable chairs in a random room of Rich Pond Baptist Church in Bowling Green, Kentucky.

But I distinctly remember this membership interview because—even though the four of us sat in a tight-knit circle alongside Pastor Steve—my friend Zach was completely and irretrievably asleep.[2] There we were, 36 inches away from our sweet pastor who was doing his darnedest to explain the joys and privileges of church membership. And there was Zach. Asleep.

I know. I know. Church membership can be soooooooooo booooooooooring. It just *sounds* boring. I mean, look at the boring title of this boring booklet: *What Should We Do about Members Who Won't Attend?* Really? Boring. Zzzzzzzzzzzzz.

But hang with me for a moment. Even if this booklet ends up being a bit boring, church membership isn't. In fact, I'd say that apart from faithfully preaching the gospel, there's absolutely nothing more important than for a church to practice *meaningful membership*.[3]

Meaningful membership. That's what this booklet is really about. It looks at a common occurrence—members who have stopped attending—and asks the question, "What should we do?" The answer to that question reveals whether a church's understanding of membership is meaningful or whether it's something else.

But before we get to that specific question, I need to persuade you of a few things.[4]

What Should We Say to Those Who Won't Attend?

Maybe you've never thought about it, but you have a responsibility to members in your church who are not attending. They need you to speak into their lives and call them back to fellowship with God's people. But before you do that, you need to have a clear understanding of what a church is and does—and why Christians should build their lives around the church. So the following points aren't just for those who aren't attending, they're for faithful attenders as well.

1. Meaningful Membership Is More Important Than You Think

What is church membership? It's the commitment Christians make to keep one another accountable for regularly gathering and centering their lives together on the gospel. That commitment and accountability takes on different forms in different times and places. Maybe there are membership classes and written church covenants. Maybe not. The point is, they're striving to take that commitment and accountability seriously—to make it meaningful.

Apart from faithfully preaching the gospel, there's nothing more important for a church to do than practice meaningful membership.

I don't mean to pit good things against each other, but I believe what I'm about to say reflects biblical priorities.

Meaningful membership is more important than sending missionaries to unreached peoples. Meaningful membership is more important than hosting evangelistic events in your neighborhood. It's more important than pursuing justice, hosting a successful counseling ministry, baptizing hundreds, doing fantastic and fruitful evangelism on a college campus, pursuing excellence in the arts, starting a seminary, or anything else you can think of.

I wonder what your eyebrows did as you read that paragraph. Well, give me a second to defend myself. The paragraph above lists a lot of wonderful and essential things churches *do*. But meaningful membership gets at what a church *is*, and we must *be* a church before we can *do* what the church is supposed to do.

Failing to practice meaningful membership strikes at the heart of everything a church does. A flimsy practice of church membership and discipline will weaken everything a church does, whereas a meaningful practice of membership and discipline will fortify everything a church does. Consider how meaningful membership strengthens the church by comparing the following questions:

> *A good question*: How many people have you baptized this year?
>
> *A better question*: Are those baptized people being discipled into membership? Do you know even where they are?

> *A good question*: Are you teaching your people to pursue justice?
>
> *A better question*: Are you disciplining members who live lives of outward, serious, and unrepentant injustice?

A good question: How much money do you give to evangelize unreached people across the world?

A better question: Do your shepherds know the sheep on your own membership roll?

Simply put, without membership a church can't be healthy. It might be a true church, insofar as it preaches the gospel and the same Christians regularly gather and recognize one another. But its preaching—and everything else—will be weakened.

Of course, no church is perfect. Having a membership class and practicing discipline doesn't make a church healthy in and of itself. And practicing meaningful membership doesn't cancel out the need to evangelize, pursue justice, send missionaries, and all the rest.

The Lord uses crooked sticks to make straight lines, amen? He uses weak things to shame the strong, amen? Every church is more-or-less crooked; every church is more-or-less weak. But a faithful practice of membership and discipline is one the best ways to know if a church is healthy.

Think of your church as a lightbulb hooked up to a dimmer switch in a dark room. Everything we do makes our witness brighter or darker. Practicing meaningful membership is one of the surest ways to turn that dimmer switch up; ignoring it is one of the surest ways to turn it down.

Meaningful membership is more important than you think.

2. Meaningful Membership Is Assumed throughout the Bible

There *are* proof-texts for church membership. My favorite is 1 Corinthians 5:12 where Paul asks, "For what have I to do with judging outsiders? Is it not those inside the church whom you are to judge?" In this single verse, we see there's an inside and an outside to a church, *and* we see that our relationship with and responsibility toward those *inside* is different than our relationship with and responsibility toward those *outside*.

But forget proof-texts. Let's talk metaphors. The Bible's metaphors for the church *assume* meaningful membership. Let's take a look.[5]

A Body (1 Corinthians 12)

Okay, I'm on a strict word count so as much as I want to, I simply can't copy-and-paste 1 Corinthians 12:12–27. So go get your Bible and read those verses. What do you see? How does Paul describe the church at Corinth?

He describes it as a human body made up of its component parts—each different, yet integral; each distinct, yet vital. Notice a few things about this passage.

First, the term "member" is a biblical word (see vv. 12, 14, 18–19). Sam Walton didn't invent it. Whoever started the Masons or the Illuminati didn't invent it. The word "membership" comes from the Bible, and we should make sure our understanding of it is influenced by Scripture, not Sam's Club.

Second, we need each other. Hands need eyes, and eyes need hands. Eyes need hands to grab what they see, and hands need eyes to see what they should grab. Every member of the church is vital, and those who only *appear* insignificant are actually indispensable (v. 22).

*A Family (Ephesians 2:19;
1 Timothy 3:15; 1 Peter 4:17)*

I'm tempted to cite every time a New Testament author refers to his audience as "brothers," but I'll simply refer you to three passages in which Peter or Paul call the church "the household of God" in Ephesians 2:19; 1 Timothy 3:15; and 1 Peter 4:17.

A household isn't a building; it's a group of people. It's a family—a mom, a dad, a few kids, that great-aunt who wears too much lipstick, that cousin to whom you say every Thanksgiving, "We should get together!" even though you both know you won't meet again until the next odd-year holiday season.

So also, the church is just that—a household, a family. And what's a family made of? Members. What's more, families have boundaries—you can't just join somebody else's family without their permission. Yes, Kramer burst into Jerry's house unannounced hundreds and hundreds of times. But he wasn't in Jerry's *family*. Same for the church.

A Temple (Ephesians 2:11–22)

Again, I would encourage you to go get your Bible and read 1 Corinthians 3:16–17; 1 Peter 2:4–5; and Ephesians 2:11–22. For now, I'll just focus on Ephesians 2.

In Ephesians 2:1–10, Paul explains how individuals are saved—"by grace . . . through faith," not by works, "so that no one may boast." As such, we are God's workmanship (v. 10). He then goes on to explain what kind of work he's building. If Ephesians 2:1–10 describes the individual bricks, then Ephesians 2:11–22 describes the *building*—and it's a spectacular one. Consider how Paul describes the church in the verses that follow:

- *Christ* has brought us near (v. 13).
- *He* is our peace (v. 14).
- *He* has created *in himself* one new man, where there were once two (v. 15).
- Where there was once hostility between us, *he* has brought peace and reconciliation (vv. 15–16).

- *He* has made us fellow citizens of a new territory: the household of God (there's that family metaphor again!). This family home is built on a foundation of true gospel doctrine, and its cornerstone is Christ himself (vv. 19–20).
- This house Jesus is building will grow into a holy temple, where God dwells with man by the Spirit (vv. 21–22).

These verses are chock-full of metaphors. We're citizens; we're family members; we're bricks in a "whole structure" (v. 21).

Now let's go a step further. In all these metaphors Scripture presents the church as an institution that's defined by its closeness and interconnectedness. It's *not* characterized primarily by its outward posture to an unbelieving world but by an essential interdependence of its component parts—that is, its component people.

Furthermore, these metaphors are *alive*. Bodies are alive. Families are alive. Even this "whole structure" in Ephesians 2:21 seems to be alive. In verse 21, Paul describes it as something that *grows* and becomes a dwelling place for the living God by the Spirit.

When you think of the church, what images come to your mind? An org chart? A cavernous, empty building? A lit-up stage? Your favorite small group, or the ministry you've served in for years? That mission trip you go on with your kids every summer?

When biblical authors think of the church—and dare I say when Jesus instituted the church—they thought of none of that, at least not primarily. They thought of a family and the members who make it up. They thought of a body, made up of all its interconnected parts. They thought of a building, but one that is *alive* because each individual brick is indwelt by the Spirit of the living God.

When we let the biblical images of the church steep in our minds, our instincts about what a church is and does ought to change. Like a steeping cup of tea, they ought to get stronger, more flavorful.[6] These instincts, then, ought to shape which actions we deem plausible or implausible. So if you view church as an org chart or your favorite small group or your most fruitful weekday ministry or whatever happens on stage or your favorite mission trip—then something like "disciplining non-attenders" will seem implausible, invasive, strange, even cruel.

But when you think about the church in the way the Bible does—as unified and alive, as redeemed persons who now comprise a redeemed people—then I suspect it won't seem so implausible or invasive or strange or cruel but rather plausible, expected, righteous, and even kind.

Put simply, a lone-ranger Christian— a Christian who lives apart from regular fellowship with a local church—may be a possibility. But it's a sad and undesirable one.

I want you to envision something: a severed hand or a loose eyeball. If that's too grisly for you, envision something else such as a woman who hasn't talked to her family in years. If that's too emotionally close to home for you, try envisioning something that couldn't possibly upset you—a brick, all by itself, sitting in a field.

A lone-ranger Christian is like that hand or eyeball or the estranged family member or that brick by itself in a field. It's sad. It's useless. It's a little bit alarming.

3. Meaningful Membership Is Both Rarer Than You Think and Easier Than You Think

Meaningful membership is rarer than you think. Even though lots of churches have "membership," they often simply use that word without rightly practicing what it means—like when a middle-schooler tells his girlfriend that he "loves" her. He means to say that word because he knows it's the right word to say, but he doesn't really know how to live it out.

Here are some common iterations of non-meaningful membership.

There's *membership-as-sentimental-attachment*. This is characterized by sentimental attachment to the church you either love or used to love the most. You know what I'm talking about. You're chatting with someone at Starbucks, and you ask him where he goes to church. He says, "Oh, I got baptized at Redeemer Baptist, just down the road." That baptism could have been last week or last century, but in that person's mind that's "his church" because he grew up there or had a meaningful spiritual experience there, even though he rarely if ever attends. In some cases, these people aren't even *members* of these churches, they just think they are. But in many cases they are members, and they will be until they die. At which point—who knows?—they might be fortunate enough to return for their funerals.

There is also *membership-as-door-opener*. Here's what I mean: a church with this sort of non-meaningful membership has membership. Perhaps they even have a membership class in which the pastor talks about the history of the church, its beliefs, and the various ministries members can be a part of. What they *don't* talk about is how membership changes the nature of both your relationship to the church and the church's relationship to you. It's never about accountability and commitment, only about opportunity. Basically, in churches like these, membership is the perfunctory step you have to take in order for you to serve in the nursery or sit on a committee or half-heartedly tap a djembe on stage every third Sunday morning.

Finally, there's *membership-as-a-programmatic-organizing-principle*. In these churches membership comes across as vitally important. They might even have a fancy name for it: "partners" or something like that. But again, the church doesn't emphasize how joining changes the status of your relationship to the church or the church's relationship to you. In these churches, membership is simply a "best practice," a means for church leaders to know their prospective financial supporters and volunteers. It enables them to "check the books," as it were, so that they can answer questions like: "What percentage of our church is giving?" Or: "What percentage of our church is serving in the nursery?" Or: "What percentage of our church attends at least once a month?" All vital questions. But when asked apart from other aspects of meaningful membership, this kind of membership falls short.

To summarize, meaningful membership is *rarer* than you think because churches often mean to practice it but fail. They make it all about opportunity or information and decidedly *not* about authority and accountability, both of which lie at the heart of what membership is. At the same time, meaningful membership is *easier* than you think because it doesn't require a ridiculously long process but simply an acknowledgement of those two neglected aspects: commitment and accountability.

Put another way, your church's membership needs to have *teeth*. It needs to reckon with the authority that is intrinsic in church membership; it's not mere sentimental attachment or an organizing principle. When you become a church member, your relationship with a certain subgroup of Christians is redefined. Remember, that's the point of 1 Corinthians 5:12. That single verse teaches both commitment and accountability.

4. Meaningful Membership Cannot Be a One-Way Street

Church membership isn't like those dread-inducing push notifications on your iPhone—

you can't opt-in and opt-out at your leisure. Let me illustrate what I mean by contrasting what I'm saying with one popular American church's understanding of membership. Here's what this church's website says in response to the question, "Does your church have membership?"

> Here at _____, we want you to know that the moment you walk through the doors, you belong here and can consider this place your church home, no title needed. Since we don't have traditional membership, you won't be able to "join" the church as a "member"—but we hope you become fully engaged in the life of the church. You can engage with us through serving strategically, connecting in a group, inviting others, and giving systematically. Those who are fully engaged with us are considered our members.

"Birkley Hills"

This paragraph is a pristine example of "membership-as-a-one-way-street," which is a first cousin with "membership-as-door-opener."

It's membership that's been evacuated of any and all commitment and accountability. It's drive-thru membership, entirely optional and entirely individualistic. It hands authority over to anyone who wants it, and leaves those who *don't* want it no better off.

What gets lost in such an approach is significant. The line between the church and the world vanishes as the church becomes entirely opt-in and self-determined. Do you consider *yourself* "fully engaged"? If so, then you *are considered* a member. As a grammar nerd, I find the passive construction extremely illuminating. No one actually does the considering in that statement!

I'm thankful that this particular church preaches the gospel. I recognize it's structured this way to buck against a wrong-headed exclusivity and lame approaches to "traditional" membership. But such a structure, even as it means to promote good things, cultivates an environment where, at best, immature believers stagnate or, at worst, nominal Christians anonymously come and go as they please, always and ever at the margins.

Regrettably, churches like this have catechized Christians' consciences such that discipline for non-attendance makes about as much sense as following the Torah's dietary laws. In fact, if you'd told me ten years ago that I'd be writing a book on church membership I would have wondered what crazy cult I'd joined and what kind of Kool-Aid they served.[7]

Some churches *have been* wrongly exclusive—mean, even. They're not salt and light; they're salty (as in, "angry") and so bright that when you look at them you wince.

But the answer to that problem is not to jettison formal commitment and accountability altogether. As a friend of mine says, "To belong before you believe is to redefine the church."[8] Instead, churches must be the right kind of exclusive—exclusive to the glory of God and for the love of all people.

We shouldn't respond to mean-spirited or dunderheaded exclusivity with naive and equally dunderheaded inclusivity. The world *needs* churches who practice meaningful membership. And not just "the world" in abstract, but the world as made up by the millions of individuals who don't know Jesus—the world as defined by your neighbors and your parents and your siblings and your children, people whose names you know. *These people* need churches who know that meaningful membership is best for them, even if they've never walked through the door.

What You're Missing

So as you think about folks in your own church who may not be attending regularly, consider what they're missing. They're missing out on the love of fellow believers. They're missing out on encouraging the body of Christ and being encouraged by the body of Christ. They're missing out on serving and being served. They're missing out on pastoral care. They're missing out on spiritual vitality that comes from being vitally connected to the body of Christ. They're missing out on obedience to Jesus.

They're a brick, an eyeball, an estranged cousin. This is a bad thing. Perhaps you and others in your church could tell them that.

What Should We Do When Members Won't Attend?

So far, I've had one goal: to tweak your understanding of what a church actually *is*. It is its members. I'm trying to shape your instincts so that you will read what comes next with open ears and eyes.

Now I want to tell a story.

A few years back, I heard about a church that had grown concerned about their bloated membership. After years of lackadaisical accounting, the number had become unwieldy, even disingenuous. Their "official" membership tallied more than twice the average attendance—doubtlessly inflated by the dead, the derelict, and the well-intentioned-but-never-there.

This discrepancy obscured the church's identity. What *was* the church? They couldn't quite say.

So the elders came up with an idea: let's just zero out the membership and, over the course of time, let those who are still around renew their commitment and rejoin the church.

This approach, they thought, would slay two giants with one smooth stone. First, it would give the church an opportunity to reach out to everyone on their list and hopefully re-invigorate the desire of some to gather with God's people. Second, they'd finally know the souls over which they were to keep watch, the individuals for whom they would one day be held accountable.

Over the course of a few months, they reached out to everyone and let them know of a date in the future when all who were willing would rededicate their spiritual oversight to this specific church. For many, doing so was a no-brainer; they'd never stopped attending. For others, God used the correspondence to pry them out of their apathy and into the pew. Hallelujah!

But for some, the letters were returned to sender (or were ignored), the emails bounced (or were ignored), and the pleas for reunion fell on deaf ears, if they fell on any ears at all.

And so, before long, their covenant with this church was deleted with a keystroke.

I submit that what happened at this church, though full of good intentions, is pastoral malpractice. It flips Jesus's parable of the lost sheep in Matthew 18 upside down: If a man has a hundred sheep, and ninety-nine of them have come back, does he not stay with the ninety-nine and leave the one alone?

It's good to have an accurate membership roll. But it's best to pursue these non-attenders toward a specific end: removal if they're attending another gospel-preaching church, restoration if they're happy to return, or excommunication if they're either unwilling to attend church anywhere or unable to be found.

In fact, I want to up the ante a bit: pursuing longstanding non-attenders (I don't mean *inconsistent* attenders, but those who have been wholly absent for several months or even years) and disciplining those who can't be found is a mark of a healthy church. Of course such pursuits can be done poorly and with a heavy hand. But this abuse should make us cautious and kind, not convinced the better choice is to do nothing. That's the central argument of this booklet.

This practice is entirely in accord with the Bible's teaching on what a church is, what a pastor is, and what biblical love is. Even if the non-attending member has no idea any pursuit or eventual discipline is happening, the church's act appropriately warns those who *are* present about the dangers of pursuing the Christian life outside a local church—about the danger of being a severed hand, an estranged aunt, or a lone brick in a field.

I've never met a growing and mature Christian who wasn't committed to a gospel-preaching church. On the other hand, I've met dozens and dozens of professing Christians who never (or sparingly) attend church. Have you? I'm sure you have. Such people's lives are an experiment in spiritual subsistence farming. They're not living in open immorality, but their confidence in their own profession of faith wavers by the day, as their last time regularly in communion with

God and under the preaching of the word floats further and further away. They'd probably never admit it, but they're becoming incredulous even at themselves.

I suppose I could have said this earlier, but I used to be a member of the church in this story. Years later, I remain deeply grateful for it, as God saved me there and discipled me under its ministry.

And yet, I struggle not to be frustrated. As I type this, so many faces flicker in my mind, faces of friends who attended church with me. We went to youth group together, to summer camp together, to accountability group together. We were young and mischievous and stupid, but we were also trying to become serious, mindful, and genuine Christians.

Then college came, and our lives meandered. Some went here; others went there; still others went nowhere. Sure, they started at one church, and then another, and then another. But after a while, their erratic commitment became non-commitment, and their non-commitment became lethargy, and their lethargy became paralysis, and their paralysis eventually started to look like death—that flicker of mindfulness had finally been snuffed out through well-intentioned inattention. As the years have passed, I wish I'd said more about this to them. Lord, please forgive me.

Once upon a time, all these friends' names were on a church membership list that said they'd spend eternity with Jesus. More than a decade later, this fact might seem incidental, detached from any substantive evidence, dismissible on a technicality or the statute of limitations.

But that's wrong. Every name was written down on purpose—the result of a sober-minded decision that Jesus is indeed the Christ, the Son of the Living God, their Lord and Savior. This decision preceded a baptism in the name of the Father, Son, and Holy Spirit.

I don't know if any of my friends got a letter or an email, and if they did, I don't know if they ignored it. But I do know what happened next: their covenant was deleted with a keystroke.

Oh, how I wish someone had warned them what that meant.

Back to the Bible

Okay, story time's over. Let's go back to the Bible and see if we can find a few passages that apply to the question at hand: Should we really discipline those who don't come to church?

Text #1: Matthew 18:10–35

If you don't have your Bible, go grab it. You need to read Matthew 18:10–35 before we continue.

What we find in this passage is that church discipline emerges from Jesus's teaching on how the Lord pursues the lost and wayward. As one pastor summarized it, "In the Bible, church discipline is a rescue operation."[9]

Notice that just before Jesus teaches about church discipline in Matthew 18:15–20 he tells the parable of the lost sheep (Matt. 18:12–14). Jesus wants to put us in the sandals of a shepherd who has lost a single sheep. His parable raises a question: What do we do if the stubborn sheep refuses to come back? Jesus answers this question in his next block of teaching: we pursue him, and if he persists in his departure, then we cast him out, treating him like a pagan and a tax collector. In other words, our relationship to the departing sheep essentially changes.

Excommunicating someone who has stopped attending is, in effect, giving them what they've asked for. It's letting go of the rope they're trying to pull out of our hands. It's not forcing them to remain bound when they don't want to be. At the same time, it's also refusing to let them force us to declare them a "Christian in good standing" when, in good conscience, we don't think we can.

For those reading closely, this raises another question: What if the sheep comes back? Jesus seems to answer that question with another parable, this one concerning an unforgiving servant (Matt. 18:21–35). The point here is simple: we lavishly forgive those who have sinned against us. Why? Because we've been forgiven by the God whom we've sinned against, an offense far more severe than whatever we've endured.

In other words, churches should quickly, gladly, and wholly forgive returning and repentant sheep because we know we ourselves have strayed and, if not for God's tether on us, we'd stray again and again, farther and farther. Mirroring David in Psalm 23, this hymn describes the lot of us:

> Perverse and foolish oft I strayed,
> But yet in love He sought me,
> And on His shoulder gently laid,
> And home rejoicing brought me.[10]

In summary, Matthew 18 teaches us both the foundation and trajectory of church discipline: we pursue straying church members because God pursues lost sheep, even if it's "just" one of ninety-nine. Sadly, this will occasionally result in exclusion because some lost sheep intend to stay lost. On these occasions, we give them what they ask for and let them go, but we insist on speaking honestly as they do, reminding them that they have no reason to consider themselves a follower of Jesus.

Happily, however, lost sheep also have a way of coming back—and when they do, we should forgive them swiftly and completely because God in Christ has forgiven us swiftly and completely.

Text #2: Hebrews 10:23–25

> Let us hold fast the confession of our hope without wavering, for he who promised is faithful. And let us consider how to stir up one another to love and good works, not neglecting to meet together, as is the habit of some, but encouraging one another, and all the more as you see the Day drawing near. (Heb. 10:23–25)

The author of Hebrews has two commands for us. The first is in verse 23: "Hold fast to the confession of our hope," a confession he's just spelled out for us by extolling what Christ accomplished as our high priest. This command is rooted in the faithfulness of God.

The second command—"stir up one another to love and good works"—is accompanied by an immediate application. How do we do this? Simple. We keep on meeting together.[11] Why? Because you can't encourage someone you never see. Again, the author roots this command and its application in a promise: we gather and encourage and spur on because we see judgment day drawing near, when our faithful, promise-keeping God will return, and we will gather with him, forever.

Though these words are nearly two-millennia old, the author of Hebrews seems familiar with our modern predicament. Did you notice? "Not neglecting to meet together, *as is the habit of some*" (v. 25).

I'm sure you know some folks who make a habit of neglecting to meet together. In doing so, they miss out on encouragement; they miss out on being spurred on to love and good works. But that's not all. Their vantage point on God's work in the Christian life shrinks, their confidence in their own confession of hope wanes, their memory of God keeping his promises fades, and their once clear-eyed vision of the coming day of the Lord begins to blur to black.

We're tempted to think skipping church is no big deal. But did you notice how severe this warning is? He mentioned "the Day [of judgment] drawing near" (v. 25). He's *that* concerned about these non-attenders that he's reminding them of God's eternal judgment. Do we take non-attendance as seriously as this Spirit-inspired author? If we do, then how can removing someone from membership for non-attendance possibly be too severe?

I keep asking you to imagine things. I promise this is the last time: Imagine a non-attending "church member" arrives at judgment day and, to his surprise, he's told he will receive God's eternal judgment. Amid this man's protestations—*But I'm a church member! But I tithed! But I . . .*—I wonder if the Lord might say, "Depart from me, for I never knew you." At this moment, how "loving" will the church seem that did nothing? How "loving" will it seem to have quietly deleted this man's name?

This man has no right to be mad at God, but he has some right to be angry at "his" church: *Why didn't you warn me?*

Who knows? Perhaps our mere, two-dimensional action of discipline *now* may be the most loving thing we can do because it warns people of the potential *permanent* reality of judgment to come.

I love these verses in Hebrews because they enable us to pursue non-attending members with our Bibles open to a chapter and verse—a proof-text!—rather than a list of well-intentioned, thought-through "I wish you woulds." We can not only point to their violation of a biblical command but also to the God-ordained benefits they're missing and the God-ordained punishment they might one day unexpectedly face.

Text #3: Hebrews 13:17

As he approaches the end of his sermon,[12] the author of Hebrews exhorts his audience:

> Obey your leaders and submit to them, for they are keeping watch over your souls, as those who will have to give an account. Let them do this with joy and not with groaning, for that would be of no advantage to you. (Heb. 13:17)

A few verses earlier, in verse 7, these leaders are described as those who "spoke to you the word of God." We're told to imitate these leaders' faith and consider the outcome of their way of life.

One implication of these verses is that church leaders should live amid their people such that the ways and outcomes of their lives can be considered and therefore imitated. Any elder who lives in an ivory tower, above and away from his people, is living below his station. Thundering commands and exhortations from the clouds, this so-called elder doesn't realize his people can't even hear him. He's talking to himself.

We should learn something from these commands. A church member who only hears from their pastors when they've done something wrong—like, say, not attend church for a year—offers a reasonable (though not foolproof) objection when they ask, "Well, where were you when the stuff that caused me to leave happened?" It's simultaneously easier *and* more effective to pastor someone on their way out the door rather than someone who's already left.

But let's get to how these verses apply to the topic at hand. Did you notice why we should obey our leaders? We should obey our leaders—assuming they're joyful and not grumbling, assuming they're qualified and live among their people—because one day *they* will give an account for *us*.

Elders have this unique responsibility. On the last day, they will give an account for every member placed under their care. If you're an elder at a church whose membership roll has no bearing in reality, then you should wonder what this means for you. If you're leading a church that has assured, through baptism and/or membership, hundreds or even thousands of people that they'll spend eternity with Jesus, but you've absolutely no idea where several of these people are, then you should at least *wonder* what this means for you. Perhaps you should also start to worry.

Paul's farewell to the Ephesian elders makes this same point: "Pay careful attention to yourselves and to all the flock, in which the Holy Spirit has made you overseers, to care for the church of God, which he obtained with his own blood" (Acts 20:28).

There's never a moment when an elder can say about a church member: *Oh, he's not my responsibility anymore.* Why? Because our Lord charges them with paying careful attention to *all* the flock—whether they're there or not, whether they want to be cared for or not.

Every member of every local church should be precious to every church leader because every member is precious to God. We shouldn't be surprised by this. After all, look at their purchase price.

Practical Steps Moving Forward

The biblical case is clear. We should pursue absent church members for at least three reasons:

- God pursues straying sheep (Matt. 18:12).
- We're told not to forsake gathering with our brothers and sisters. This isn't an optional command (Heb. 10:25).

- Our elders will give account to God for every single person placed under their care. There are no exceptions (Heb. 13:17).

So the Bible makes these points. Now what? That's a good question. No church or pastor should read this booklet and start to discipline non-attenders tomorrow.[13] It will take time to recalibrate a church's conscience, filter out bad assumptions, and inject better ones.

So don't start immediately. But over time, consider the following building steps. This next section is geared more toward church leaders, those who have their hands on a church's decision-making levers.

1. In your church covenant, add a line or two that mentions what members should do when they leave.

My former church used this line: "We will, when we move from this place, as soon as possible, unite with some other church where we can carry out the spirit of this covenant and the principles of God's Word." Brief, general, and to-the-point—that should be the goal.

Of course, the words in your church covenant won't matter if it just gathers dust. So use it: in membership classes, when you take the Lord's Supper, before you begin members' meetings, periodically in your sermon application.

I'd say the same should be true of your church's constitution. Tighten it up with language that doesn't just allow members to resign their membership unilaterally.[14]

2. Teach your members about their God-given authority and responsibility.

We've already talked about our need to reclaim the Bible's categories of commitment and accountability. This reclamation needs to be congregation-wide, not just felt by a majority of its leadership.

Why? Because church discipline starts with every church member (Matt. 18:15). Thankfully, the process usually stops after step 1, when Member A gently confronts Member B, and Member B responds in gratitude and repentance.

But on those unfortunate occasions when a sinning member remains unrepentant, it's important to underscore the whole church's involvement. A steady diet of teaching on this will help people see that, just like their elders, they have no reason to say that a church member is no longer their concern. The pursuit of an absent member is a congregational project; it's not just for those who are paid or elected to care.

3. Don't be territorial.
Speak well of other churches.

I've often heard that excommunicating non-attending members is spiritually abusive, that it's evidence of a territorial ungodliness or a lust for market control. I suppose this is hypothetically possible, but I don't know of anyone who thinks doing this will help them in the short-term. Just the opposite, in fact, pastors more than anyone know it may prove difficult and costly.

Further, a charge like this simply won't stick to churches that are known for their big-heartedness. So regularly send members to help other churches. Share your pulpit. Plant churches without your particular branding or ecclesiological imprimatur. Pray for other churches publicly. Don't be a denominational shill. Build cooperative friendships with gospel-preaching churches across denominational lines.

4. Teach on the derivative authority of the church.

Your church and its members have real, God-given authority, which means we must exercise it soberly and carefully. Passages like Matthew 18:15–20 and 1 Corinthians 5 are clear: the decisions we make when we gather *mean something*.

But we must never forget: our authority, though derived from the Lord, is not analogous to his. Instead, when we teach on the church's authority, we must stress that it's real, but that's it's also derivative, limited, and potentially errant.

Perhaps that member you can't find and haven't heard from moved last-minute and, as we all sometimes do, forgot to tell anyone. Perhaps their AOL or Earthlink.net account finally went the way of the dodo. Perhaps they're gladly serving in another church across the country. I'd guess these situations will be the minority, but they will happen, which is why we must constantly teach people that an excommunication for non-attendance is *not* a declaration that member X has been cut off from the Lord. It's simply a declaration that, despite our best efforts, we don't know where he or she is, and therefore we must withdraw our affirmation of their profession of faith.

Do What's Best for Non-Christians and Fake Christians

Okay, I lied. I want you to imagine one more thing: Imagine every gospel-preaching church cared for its membership like this—not with a proud attempt at perfection but with a humble attempt at honesty. Not with a helicopter parent's lack of trust, but with a pastor's heart of concern.

It would bless nominal Christians because it would warn them when evidence of their nominalism piles up. That evidence might include their non-attendance. It might be some kind of persistent, unrepentant habit that keeps them away from the gathering out of fear or shame. Such a practice would wave a caution flag as they're speeding around the racetrack of life, letting them know that though they think they're on the narrow path, they're actually on the wide one.

It would also bless self-described non-Christians because they won't see a church's witness weakened and diluted by those who claim "membership" with this-or-that church out of mere sentiment or convenience.

In such a world, don't you think non-Christians would have a better idea of what Christianity actually is? Don't you think they'd more clearly understand what it means to live as a Christian? Don't you think Jesus might be a little bit more attractive to them?

You're going to die one day. When you do, if you're a Christian, you're going to hear some glorious words: "Well done, good and faithful servant. . . . Enter into the joy of your master" (Matt. 25:23). Hallelujah!

All your friends are going to die too. And when they do, if they're not Christians, they're going to hear some gut-wrenching words, perhaps for the first time, perhaps to their utter surprise: "Depart from me, for I never knew you."

Oh, in that moment, how they will wish someone would have warned them.

Notes

1. C. H. Spurgeon, *The Sword and the Trowel; A Record of Combat with Sin & Labour for the Lord.* 37 vols. (London: Passmore & Alabaster, 1865–1902), 1872:198.
2. Personal stories involving other individuals are shared in this booklet with permission from those individuals. Sometimes pseudonyms have been used for privacy.
3. When I use the phrase "meaningful membership," discipline is implied. In a fallen world, church membership simply cannot be meaningful without the occasional practice of discipline.
4. Some of the material in this booklet is taken and adapted from Alex Duke, "Why Churches Should Excommunicate Longstanding Non-Attenders," *9Marks* website, August 14, 2020, https://www.9marks .org/article/why-churches-should-excommunicate -longstanding-non-attenders/. Used with permission of 9Marks.
5. For a helpful article on this topic, see Sam Emadi, "Metaphors and Membership: How Biblical Metaphors for

the Church Require Church Membership," *9Marks* website, May 7, 2019, https://www.9marks.org/article/metaphors-and-membership-how-biblical-metaphors-for-the-church-require-church-membership/.

6. I've never had a cup of tea, but I assume this is how it works.

7. If my childhood is any indication, probably a mixture of grape and black cherry. Also, Jim Jones actually served Flavor Aid, not Kool-Aid.

8. I'm cribbing this line from my friend Michael Lawrence.

9. Juan Sanchez, "How Can Church Discipline be Loving?" July 18, 2017, https://www.youtube.com/watch?v=-gmU23x900g.

10. Henry Williams Baker, "The King of Love My Shepherd Is," 1868.

11. On meeting together, see Sam Allberry, *Why Bother with Church?* Questions Christians Ask (The Good Book Co., 2016); or Mark Dever, "Reasons to Join a Church" (lecture 15 of the Marks of a Healthy Church teaching series by Ligonier Ministries), https://www.ligonier.org/learn/series/marks-healthy-church/reasons-join-church/.

12. Hey, I wouldn't ever know this . . . but smart people say Hebrews is a sermon, more than a letter.

13. Unless you want to get fired. In which case, Godspeed!

14. For more on this topic, check out Jonathan Leeman, "The Preemptive Resignation—A Get Out of Jail Free Card?" *9Marks* website, February 25, 2010, https://www.9marks.org/article/preemptive-resignation-get-out-jail-free-card/.

Scripture Index

IX 9Marks

Building Healthy Churches

9Marks exists to equip church leaders with a biblical vision and practical resources for displaying God's glory to the nations through healthy churches.

To that end, we want to see churches characterized by these nine marks of health:

1. Expositional Preaching
2. Gospel Doctrine
3. A Biblical Understanding of Conversion and Evangelism
4. Biblical Church Membership
5. Biblical Church Discipline
6. A Biblical Concern for Discipleship and Growth
7. Biblical Church Leadership
8. A Biblical Understanding of the Practice of Prayer
9. A Biblical Understanding and Practice of Missions

Find all our Crossway titles and other resources at 9Marks.org.

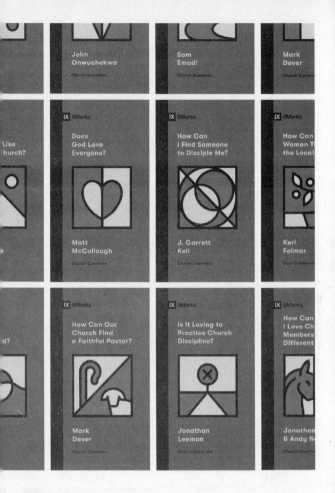

John Onwuchekwa
Church Questions

Sam Emadi
Church Questions

Mark Dever
Church Questions

...Like ...hurch?

Does God Love Everyone?
Matt McCullough
Church Questions

How Can I Find Someone to Disciple Me?
J. Garrett Kell
Church Questions

How Can Women T... the Local
Keri Folmar
Church Questions

...d?

How Can Our Church Find a Faithful Pastor?
Mark Dever
Church Questions

Is It Loving to Practice Church Discipline?
Jonathan Leeman
Church Questions

How Can I Love Ch... Members Different...
Jonathan & Andy N...
Church Questions

IX 9Marks Church Questions

Providing ordinary Christians with sound and accessible biblical teaching by answering common questions about church life.

For more information, visit crossway.org.